2023-2024
Monthly Planner

Personal Information

NAME: ___________________________

ADDRESS: ___________________________

PHONE: ___________________________

EMAIL: ___________________________

Contacts

Name: ___________________________   Name: ___________________________

Address: ___________________________   Address: ___________________________

Phone: ___________________________   Phone: ___________________________

Email: ___________________________   Email: ___________________________

Name: ___________________________   Name: ___________________________

Address: ___________________________   Address: ___________________________

Phone: ___________________________   Phone: ___________________________

Email: ___________________________   Email: ___________________________

Name: ___________________________   Name: ___________________________

Address: ___________________________   Address: ___________________________

Phone: ___________________________   Phone: ___________________________

Email: ___________________________   Email: ___________________________

Name: ___________________________   Name: ___________________________

Address: ___________________________   Address: ___________________________

Phone: ___________________________   Phone: ___________________________

Email: ___________________________   Email: ___________________________

Name: ___________________________   Name: ___________________________

Address: ___________________________   Address: ___________________________

Phone: ___________________________   Phone: ___________________________

Email: ___________________________   Email: ___________________________

Contacts

Name: _______________________

Address: _______________________

Phone: _______________________

Email: _______________________

Name: _______________________

Address: _______________________

Phone: _______________________

Email: _______________________

Name: _______________________

Address: _______________________

Phone: _______________________

Email: _______________________

Name: _______________________

Address: _______________________

Phone: _______________________

Email: _______________________

Name: _______________________

Address: _______________________

Phone: _______________________

Email: _______________________

Name: _______________________

Address: _______________________

Phone: _______________________

Email: _______________________

Name: _______________________

Address: _______________________

Phone: _______________________

Email: _______________________

Name: _______________________

Address: _______________________

Phone: _______________________

Email: _______________________

Name: _______________________

Address: _______________________

Phone: _______________________

Email: _______________________

Name: _______________________

Address: _______________________

Phone: _______________________

Email: _______________________

Contacts

Name: _______________________________

Address: _____________________________

Phone: ______________________________

Email: _______________________________

Name: _______________________________

Address: _____________________________

Phone: ______________________________

Email: _______________________________

Name: _______________________________

Address: _____________________________

Phone: ______________________________

Email: _______________________________

Name: _______________________________

Address: _____________________________

Phone: ______________________________

Email: _______________________________

Name: _______________________________

Address: _____________________________

Phone: ______________________________

Email: _______________________________

Name: _______________________________

Address: _____________________________

Phone: ______________________________

Email: _______________________________

Name: _______________________________

Address: _____________________________

Phone: ______________________________

Email: _______________________________

Name: _______________________________

Address: _____________________________

Phone: ______________________________

Email: _______________________________

Password log

Website:	**Website:**
Username:	Username:
Password:	Password:
Email:	Email:
Notes:	Notes:
Website:	**Website:**
Username:	Username:
Password:	Password:
Email:	Email:
Notes:	Notes:
Website:	**Website:**
Username:	Username:
Password:	Password:
Email:	Email:
Notes:	Notes:
Website:	**Website:**
Username:	Username:
Password:	Password:
Email:	Email:
Notes:	Notes:
Website:	**Website:**
Username:	Username:
Password:	Password:
Email:	Email:
Notes:	Notes:
Website:	**Website:**
Username:	Username:
Password:	Password:
Email:	Email:
Notes:	Notes:

Password log

<table>
<tr><td>

Website: [ ]
Username: _______________
Password: _______________
Email: _______________
Notes: _______________

</td><td>

Website: [ ]
Username: _______________
Password: _______________
Email: _______________
Notes: _______________

</td></tr>
<tr><td>

Website: [ ]
Username: _______________
Password: _______________
Email: _______________
Notes: _______________

</td><td>

Website: [ ]
Username: _______________
Password: _______________
Email: _______________
Notes: _______________

</td></tr>
<tr><td>

Website: [ ]
Username: _______________
Password: _______________
Email: _______________
Notes: _______________

</td><td>

Website: [ ]
Username: _______________
Password: _______________
Email: _______________
Notes: _______________

</td></tr>
<tr><td>

Website: [ ]
Username: _______________
Password: _______________
Email: _______________
Notes: _______________

</td><td>

Website: [ ]
Username: _______________
Password: _______________
Email: _______________
Notes: _______________

</td></tr>
<tr><td>

Website: [ ]
Username: _______________
Password: _______________
Email: _______________
Notes: _______________

</td><td>

Website: [ ]
Username: _______________
Password: _______________
Email: _______________
Notes: _______________

</td></tr>
<tr><td>

Website: [ ]
Username: _______________
Password: _______________
Email: _______________
Notes: _______________

</td><td>

Website: [ ]
Username: _______________
Password: _______________
Email: _______________
Notes: _______________

</td></tr>
</table>

Password log

Website:	Website:
Username:	Username:
Password:	Password:
Email:	Email:
Notes:	Notes:

Website:	Website:
Username:	Username:
Password:	Password:
Email:	Email:
Notes:	Notes:

Website:	Website:
Username:	Username:
Password:	Password:
Email:	Email:
Notes:	Notes:

Website:	Website:
Username:	Username:
Password:	Password:
Email:	Email:
Notes:	Notes:

Website:	Website:
Username:	Username:
Password:	Password:
Email:	Email:
Notes:	Notes:

Website:	Website:
Username:	Username:
Password:	Password:
Email:	Email:
Notes:	Notes:

Year In Review 2023

January

S	M	T	W	T	F	S
1	2	3	4	5	6	7
8	9	10	11	12	13	14
15	16	17	18	19	20	21
22	23	24	25	26	27	28
29	30	31				

February

S	M	T	W	T	F	S
			1	2	3	4
5	6	7	8	9	10	11
12	13	14	15	16	17	18
19	20	21	22	23	24	25
26	27	28				

March

S	M	T	W	T	F	S
			1	2	3	4
5	6	7	8	9	10	11
12	13	14	15	16	17	18
19	20	21	22	23	24	25
26	27	28	29	30	31	

April

S	M	T	W	T	F	S
						1
2	3	4	5	6	7	8
9	10	11	12	13	14	15
16	17	18	19	20	21	22
23	24	25	26	27	28	29
30						

May

S	M	T	W	T	F	S
	1	2	3	4	5	6
7	8	9	10	11	12	13
14	15	16	17	18	19	20
21	22	23	24	25	26	27
28	29	30	31			

June

S	M	T	W	T	F	S
				1	2	3
4	5	6	7	8	9	10
11	12	13	14	15	16	17
18	19	20	21	22	23	24
25	26	27	28	29	30	

July

S	M	T	W	T	F	S
						1
2	3	4	5	6	7	8
9	10	11	12	13	14	15
16	17	18	19	20	21	22
23	24	25	26	27	28	29
30	31					

August

S	M	T	W	T	F	S
		1	2	3	4	5
6	7	8	9	10	11	12
13	14	15	16	17	18	19
20	21	22	23	24	25	26
27	28	29	30	31		

September

S	M	T	W	T	F	S
					1	2
3	4	5	6	7	8	9
10	11	12	13	14	15	16
17	18	19	20	21	22	23
24	25	26	27	28	29	30

October

S	M	T	W	T	F	S
1	2	3	4	5	6	7
8	9	10	11	12	13	14
15	16	17	18	19	20	21
22	23	24	25	26	27	28
29	30	31				

November

S	M	T	W	T	F	S
			1	2	3	4
5	6	7	8	9	10	11
12	13	14	15	16	17	18
19	20	21	22	23	24	25
26	27	28	29	30		

December

S	M	T	W	T	F	S
					1	2
3	4	5	6	7	8	9
10	11	12	13	14	15	16
17	18	19	20	21	22	23
24	25	26	27	28	29	30
31						

Holidays & Celebrations

Jan 01	New Year's Day		Jul 04	Independence Day
Jan 16	Martin Luther King Jr. Day		Sep 04	Labor Day
Feb 14	Valentine's Day		Oct 02	Cabrini Day
Feb 20	President's Day		Oct 09	Columbus Day
Apr 09	Easter Sunday		Oct 31	Halloween
Apr 15	Tax Day		Nov 10	Veterans Day
May 14	Mother's Day		Nov 23	Thanksgiving Day
May 29	Memorial Day		Nov 24	Black Friday
Jun 18	Father's Day		Dec 25	Christmas Day
Jun 19	Juneteenth		Dec 27	Christmas Holiday

Notes

Important Dates

JANUARY

FEBRUARY

MARCH

APRIL

MAY

JUNE

JULY

AUGUST

SEPTEMBER

OCTOBER

NOVEMBER

DECEMBER

2023 Goals/ Projects

January 2023

Sunday	Monday	Tuesday	Wednesday
1	2	3	4
8	9	10	11
15	16	17	18
22	23	24	25
29	30	31	

Thursday	Friday	Saturday
5	6	7
12	13	14
19	20	21
26	27	28

February 2023

Sunday	Monday	Tuesday	Wednesday
			1
5	6	7	8
12	13	14	15
19	20	21	22
26	27	28	

Thursday	Friday	Saturday
		1
6	7	8
13	14	15
20	21	22
27	28	29

March 2023

Sunday	Monday	Tuesday	Wednesday
			1
5	6	7	8
12	13	14	15
19	20	21	22
26	27	28	29

Thursday	Friday	Saturday
2	3	4
9	10	11
16	17	18
23	24	25
30	31	

April 2023

Sunday	Monday	Tuesday	Wednesday
2	3	4	5
9	10	11	12
16	17	18	19
23	24	25	26
30			

Thursday	Friday	Saturday
		1
6	7	8
13	14	15
20	21	22
27	28	29

May 2023

Sunday	Monday	Tuesday	Wednesday
	1	2	3
7	8	9	10
14	15	16	17
21	22	23	24
28	29	30	31

Thursday	Friday	Saturday
4	5	6
11	12	13
18	19	20
25	26	27

June 2023

Sunday	Monday	Tuesday	Wednesday
4	5	6	7
11	12	13	14
18	19	20	21
25	26	27	28

Thursday	Friday	Saturday
1	2	3
8	9	10
15	16	17
22	23	24
29	30	

July 2023

Sunday	Monday	Tuesday	Wednesday
2	3	4	5
9	10	11	12
16	17	18	19
23	24	25	26
30	31		

Thursday	Friday	Saturday	
		1	
6	7	8	
13	14	15	
20	21	22	
27	28	29	

August 2023

Sunday	Monday	Tuesday	Wednesday
		1	2
6	7	8	9
13	14	15	16
20	21	22	23
27	28	29	30

Thursday	Friday	Saturday	NOTES
3	4	5	
10	11	12	
17	18	19	
24	25	26	
31			

September 2023

Sunday	Monday	Tuesday	Wednesday
3	4	5	6
10	11	12	13
17	18	19	20
24	25	26	27

Thursday	Friday	Saturday	
	1	2	**NOTES**
7	8	9	
14	15	16	
21	22	23	
28	29	30	

October 2023

Sunday	Monday	Tuesday	Wednesday
1	2	3	4
8	9	10	11
15	16	17	18
22	23	24	25
29	30	31	

Thursday	Friday	Saturday	
5	6	7	
12	13	14	
19	20	21	
26	27	28	

November 2023

Sunday	Monday	Tuesday	Wednesday
			1
5	6	7	8
12	13	14	15
19	20	21	22
26	27	28	29

<table>
<tr><td>MONTH GOALS</td><td colspan="2">TO DO LIST</td></tr>
</table>

Thursday	Friday	Saturday	NOTES
2	3	4	
9	10	11	
16	17	18	
23	24	25	
30			

December 2023

Sunday	Monday	Tuesday	Wednesday
3	4	5	6
10	11	12	13
17	18	19	20
24	25	26	27
31			

Thursday	Friday	Saturday
	1	2
7	8	9
14	15	16
21	22	23
28	29	30

Notes

Notes

# Notes

Best Memories Of The Year

Best Memories Of The Year

Best Memories Of The Year

Year In Review 2024

January

S	M	T	W	T	F	S
	1	2	3	4	5	6
7	8	9	10	11	12	13
14	15	16	17	18	19	20
21	22	23	24	25	26	27
28	29	30	31			

February

S	M	T	W	T	F	S
				1	2	3
4	5	6	7	8	9	10
11	12	13	14	15	16	17
18	19	20	21	22	23	24
25	26	27	28	29		

March

S	M	T	W	T	F	S
					1	2
3	4	5	6	7	8	9
10	11	12	13	14	15	16
17	18	19	20	21	22	23
24	25	26	27	28	29	30
31						

April

S	M	T	W	T	F	S
	1	2	3	4	5	6
7	8	9	10	11	12	13
14	15	16	17	18	19	20
21	22	23	24	25	26	27
28	29	30				

May

S	M	T	W	T	F	S
			1	2	3	4
5	6	7	8	9	10	11
12	13	14	15	16	17	18
19	20	21	22	23	24	25
26	27	28	29	30	31	

June

S	M	T	W	T	F	S
						1
2	3	4	5	6	7	8
9	10	11	12	13	14	15
16	17	18	19	20	21	22
23	24	25	26	27	28	29
30						

July

S	M	T	W	T	F	S
	1	2	3	4	5	6
7	8	9	10	11	12	13
14	15	16	17	18	19	20
21	22	23	24	25	26	27
28	29	30	31			

August

S	M	T	W	T	F	S
				1	2	3
4	5	6	7	8	9	10
11	12	13	14	15	16	17
18	19	20	21	22	23	24
25	26	27	28	29	30	31

September

S	M	T	W	T	F	S
1	2	3	4	5	6	7
8	9	10	11	12	13	14
15	16	17	18	19	20	21
22	23	24	25	26	27	28
29	30					

October

S	M	T	W	T	F	S
		1	2	3	4	5
6	7	8	9	10	11	12
13	14	15	16	17	18	19
20	21	22	23	24	25	26
27	28	29	30	31		

November

S	M	T	W	T	F	S
					1	2
3	4	5	6	7	8	9
10	11	12	13	14	15	16
17	18	19	20	21	22	23
24	25	26	27	28	29	30

December

S	M	T	W	T	F	S
1	2	3	4	5	6	7
8	9	10	11	12	13	14
15	16	17	18	19	20	21
22	23	24	25	26	27	28
29	30	31				

Holidays & Celebrations

Jan 01	New Year's Day	Jul 04	Independence Day
Jan 15	Martin Luther King Jr. Day	Sep 02	Labor Day
Feb 14	Valentine's Day	Oct 07	Cabrini Day
Feb 19	President's Day	Oct 14	Columbus Day
Apr 01	Easter Monday	Oct 31	Halloween
Apr 15	Tax Day	Nov 11	Veterans Day
May 12	Mother's Day	Nov 28	Thanksgiving Day
May 27	Memorial Day	Nov 29	Black Friday
Jun 16	Father's Day	Dec 25	Christmas Day
Jun 19	Juneteenth	Dec 31	New Years Eve 2024

Notes

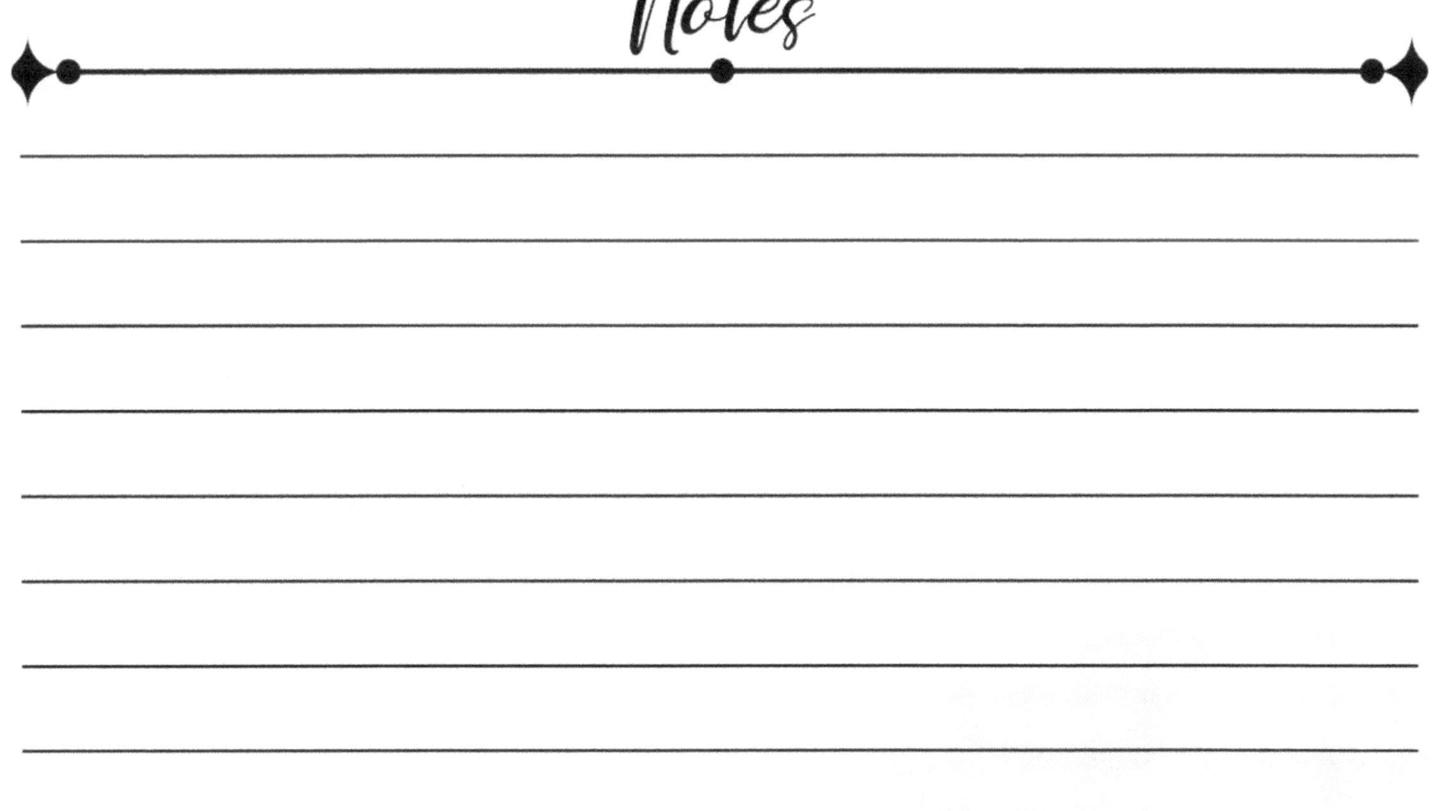

Important Dates

JANUARY	FEBRUARY

MARCH	APRIL

MAY	JUNE

JULY	AUGUST

SEPTEMBER	OCTOBER

NOVEMBER	DECEMBER

2024 Goals/ Projects

January 2024

Sunday	Monday	Tuesday	Wednesday
	1	2	3
7	8	9	10
14	15	16	17
21	22	23	24
28	29	30	31

Thursday	Friday	Saturday
4	5	6
11	12	13
18	19	20
25	26	27

February 2024

Sunday	Monday	Tuesday	Wednesday
4	5	6	7
11	12	13	14
18	19	20	21
25	26	27	28

Thursday	Friday	Saturday	
1	2	3	
8	9	10	
15	16	17	
22	23	24	
29			

March 2024

Sunday	Monday	Tuesday	Wednesday
3	4	5	6
10	11	12	13
17	18	19	20
24	25	26	27
31			

<table>
<tr><th colspan="2" style="background:#808080;color:white;text-align:center">MONTH GOALS</th><th colspan="2" style="background:#808080;color:white;text-align:center">TO DO LIST</th></tr>
</table>

Thursday	Friday	Saturday	NOTES
	1	2	
7	8	9	
14	15	16	
21	22	23	
28	29	30	

April 2024

Sunday	Monday	Tuesday	Wednesday
	1	2	3
7	8	9	10
14	15	16	17
21	22	23	24
28	29	30	

Thursday	Friday	Saturday	NOTES
4	5	6	
11	12	13	
18	19	20	
25	26	27	

May 2024

Sunday	Monday	Tuesday	Wednesday
			1
5	6	7	8
12	13	14	15
19	20	21	22
26	27	28	29

Thursday	Friday	Saturday
2	3	4
9	10	11
16	17	18
23	24	25
30	31	

June 2024

Sunday	Monday	Tuesday	Wednesday
2	3	4	5
9	10	11	12
16	17	18	19
23	24	25	26
30			

Thursday	Friday	Saturday
		1
6	7	8
13	14	15
20	21	22
27	28	29

July 2024

Sunday	Monday	Tuesday	Wednesday
	1	2	3
7	8	9	10
14	15	16	17
21	22	23	24
28	29	30	31

Thursday	Friday	Saturday	NOTES
4	5	6	
11	12	13	
18	19	20	
25	26	27	

August 2024

Sunday	Monday	Tuesday	Wednesday
4	5	6	7
11	12	13	14
18	19	20	21
25	26	27	28

Thursday	Friday	Saturday
1	2	3
8	9	10
15	16	17
22	23	24
29	30	31

September 2024

Sunday	Monday	Tuesday	Wednesday
1	2	3	4
8	9	10	11
15	16	17	18
22	23	24	25
29	30		

<table>
<tr><td>MONTH GOALS</td><td>TO DO LIST</td></tr>
</table>

Thursday	Friday	Saturday	NOTES
5	6	7	
12	13	14	
19	20	21	
26	27	28	

October 2024

Sunday	Monday	Tuesday	Wednesday
		1	2
6	7	8	9
13	14	15	16
20	21	22	23
27	28	29	30

Thursday	Friday	Saturday	NOTES
3	4	5	
10	11	12	
17	18	19	
24	25	26	
31			

November 2024

Sunday	Monday	Tuesday	Wednesday
3	4	5	6
10	11	12	13
17	18	19	20
24	25	26	27

Thursday	Friday	Saturday
	1	2
7	8	9
14	15	16
21	22	23
28	29	30

December 2024

Sunday	Monday	Tuesday	Wednesday
1	2	3	4
8	9	10	11
15	16	17	18
22	23	24	25
29	30	31	

Thursday	Friday	Saturday
5	6	7
12	13	14
19	20	21
26	27	28

Notes

Best Memories Of The Year

Best Memories Of The Year

Best Memories Of The Year

Notes

Notes